CARTA's HISTORICAL ATLAS OF JERUSALEM
A Brief Illustrated Survey

Dan Bahat

Carta, The Israel Map & Publishing Co. Ltd., Jerusalem

TABLE OF CONTENTS

First published in Hebrew 1970
First English edition 1973
Charles Scribner's Sons edition 1975
Revised and expanded 1976

Printed in Israel

FOREWORD

Like any really great subject, the city of Jerusalem can be dealt with at any length. The "Petit Larousse" devotes to it just six and a half lines. P. P. Abel and Vincent have written seven volumes on its history and legacy, G. A. Smith two volumes and G. Dalman one.

D a n   B a h a t, for his part, has rendered yeoman service to all those desirous of studying step by step the constructional and architectural development of the Holy City. In this book, he has summed up in a very short space and in a highly visual manner the main facts relevant to his subject, while availing himself of the results of the latest excavations and researches. He has thus undoubtedly earned the gratitude of the many students who wish to acquaint themselves with the city's past, the better to understand its present and future. For those inclined to pursue this study further, this little atlas will certainly serve as a reliable introduction and as an initiation into the love of Jerusalem.

Michael Avi-Yonah

"... the mountains are round about Jerusalem" Psalms II 125, 2

The Topography of Ancient Jerusalem

Indeed Jerusalem is situated in the heart of the Judean mountains on the watershed between the fertile plains and the Judean Desert.

The ancient city of Jerusalem extended over two hills: the hill of the City of David and the Temple Mount where ancient Jerusalem was first built and the western hills and Mt. Zion along which Jerusalem spread in the Second Temple period.

The two hills are separated by a deep dale called the Tyropoeon (erroneously translated Cheesemakers' Valley) which drains the rainwater from the mountain city into the Kidron Valley. To the east the city is cut off from its surroundings by the Kidron Valley which runs from north to south and is banked on the east by the Mt. of Olives (830m) which is higher than Jerusalem itself (Temple Mount, 744m). To the south is the Hinnom Valley which too is deep and limits easy access to the city. Some lesser riverbeds in the close vicinity of the town have also influenced the city's development.

Low gently sloping hills skirt the city to the north and west, and there no natural barrier cuts Jerusalem off from its surroundings.

Kenyon's main trench on Ophel Hill.

The Canaanite, Jebusite and Israelite Periods

−586 B.C.E.)

Two major sources throw light on the countenance of Jerusalem during this lengthy period. The first is the Bible; although it contains no complete description of the Jerusalem of the First Temple days, one can get some picture of the city from the bits and pieces of information in its various books. The most important in this connection is the Book of Nehemiah which, although written later, partially describes the situation as it was prior to the Destruction of the First Temple. Three episodes bear directly on the physical features of Jerusalem: Nehemiah's night-time reconnaissance of the city walls after returning from the Babylonian Exile (Neh. 2, 11–15); the construction of the city walls (Neh. 3, 1–32); and the thanksgiving ceremony on the completion of the walls (Neh. 12, 31–41). There are in addition many other fragmentary references to Jerusalem in the Bible such as David's capture and building of Jerusalem (Sam. II:5, 4–12); Solomon's extensive construction-work (Kings I:6, 7, 9, 10–15); Hezekiah's conduit bringing water into the city and the wall he built around the Siloam Pool (Chron. II:32, 3–5; Kings II:20, 20); and Jerusalem in the days of Manasseh (Chron. II: 23, 14).

These verses, of course, supply a partial picture only. That Jerusalem extended over the south-east ridge of the Ophel Mount (the "City of David") is accepted by all the scholars, but some reckon that it extended over the south-west ridge as well (Mt. Zion and the area of the Jewish and Armenian Quarters)—a view given further credibility by recent excavations. It seems that the south-west hill constituted a suburb of Jerusalem but until the mid 8th century B.C.E. had not been fortified to the same extent as the heart of the city itself.

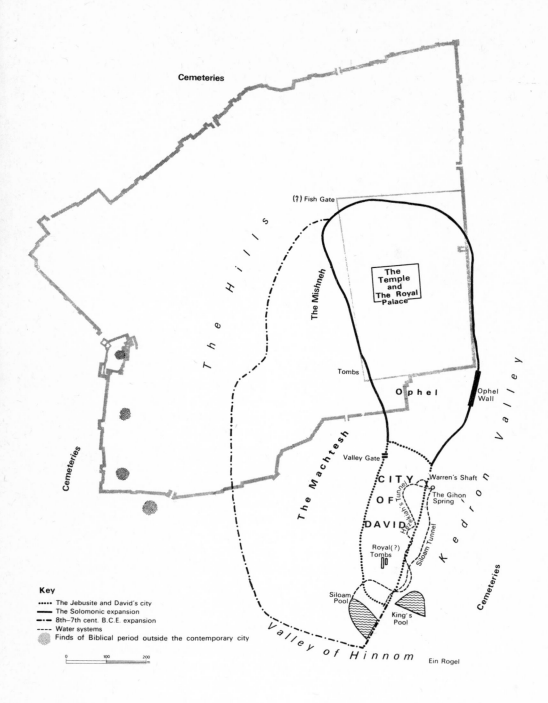

Cemeteries

The Hills

Cemeteries

(?) Fish Gate

The Mishneh

The
Temple
and
The Royal
Palace

Tombs

Ophel

Ophel
Wall

Kedron Valley

The Machtesh

Valley Gate

Warren's Shaft

CITY
OF
DAVID

Hezekiah's Tunnel

The Gihon
Spring

Siloam Tunnel

Royal(?)
Tombs

Siloam
Pool

King's
Pool

Cemeteries

Valley of Hinnom

Ein Rogel

Key

····· The Jebusite and David's city
───── The Solomonic expansion
─·─·─ 8th–7th cent. B.C.E. expansion
----- Water systems
◯ Finds of Biblical period outside the contemporary city

0   100   200
                m

7

Nobleman's tomb of the First Temple period in the village of Siloam. Known as the "Tomb of Pharoah's Daughter."

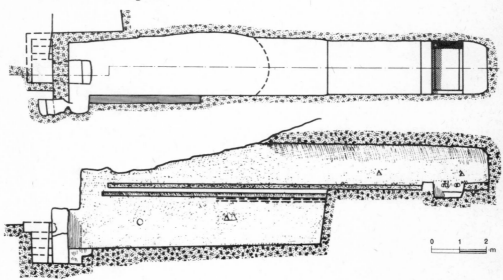

THE WEILL TOMBS. Among the most famous excavations carried out on the Ophel Ridge were those of R. Weill in 1913–14 and in 1923–24. In the course of his excavations here, Weill discovered what he believed to be tomb complexes. Because they had been broken into in Roman times and all their contents had been stolen, it was difficult to determine their exact purpose, but Weill believed them to have been the tombs of the House of David.

The above tomb consists of a passage about 16 metres long ending in a depression in which the sarcophagus presumably reposed. When, after some years, the cemetery became overcrowded, other graves were dug out below the surface of the passage, and, with the aid of two fissures cut along the length of its original floor, a wooden platform was installed along which it was possible to cross from the entrance to the grave at the far end.

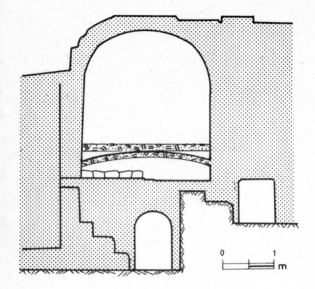

Northern view of the Weill Tomb. The main archway leads to the large grave, while the small arch is the opening of a grave added later, and which was reached by means of steps leading downwards. It has been suggested to restore the wooden girders which supported the floor of the large grave.

The second source to contribute to our picture of Jerusalem is arc aeology. Jerusalem always proved a prime attraction to archaeologists from the very outset of archaeological research in the Holy Land. The explorers always concentrated their major efforts on Mt. Ophel.

Kathleen Kenyon's excavations from 1961 to 1968 and Ruth Amiran's dig in the Citadel indicate that the Armenian Quarter was already a residential area during the First Temple period. But this area was probably outside the contemporary city walls which have been discovered in the Jewish Quarter. Prof. Avigad's excavations there indicate that from the eighth century to the Destruction of the First Temple in 586 B.C.E. by Nebuchadnezzar the Chaldean, Jerusalem was a strongly fortified city with a large population; at this time it extended over the south-eastern slopes of Mount Zion and into the present-day Jewish Quarter. A very broad wall—the most sturdy of all the First Temple walls discovered in the country—formed the western confines of the city.

The excavations also turned up evidence of various water systems; the most famous find was the inscription of Hezekiah's tunnel which describes the boring of the water tunnel from the Gihon Spring to the Pool of Siloam which during Hezekiah's reign was already included within the newly built wall. The inscription is now in the Museum at Istanbul.

The accompanying map shows the city boundaries on the Ophel, as reconstructed from small sections of the city wall which have been discovered.

The temple and palace on the Temple Mount were originally surrounded by a wall, none of which has been uncovered as Herod had it destroyed when he rebuilt the Temple and the Temple Mount enclosure. The course of the wall represented on the map is determined by the topography of the terrain as it is presumed that the wall skirted the Temple Mount summit.

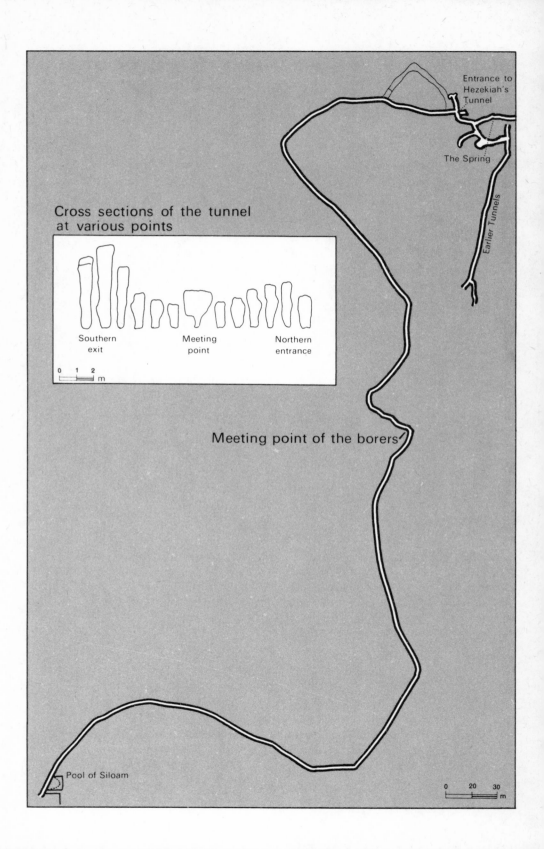

Cross sections of the tunnel
at various points

Southern
exit

Meeting
point

Northern
entrance

0 1 2
m

Meeting point of the borers

Entrance to
Hezekiah's
Tunnel

The Spring

Earlier Tunnels

Pool of Siloam

0   20   30
m

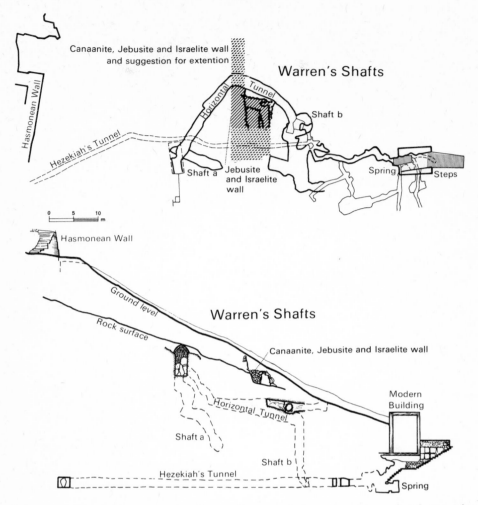

Warren's Shafts

Canaanite, Jebusite and Israelite wall and suggestion for extention

Horizontal Tunnel

Shaft b

Shaft a

Jebusite and Israelite wall

Spring

Steps

Hasmonean Wall

Hezekiah's Tunnel

0   5   10
m

Hasmonean Wall

Ground level

Rock surface

Warren's Shafts

Canaanite, Jebusite and Israelite wall

Modern Building

Horizontal Tunnel

Shaft a

Shaft b

Hezekiah's Tunnel

Spring

KENYON'S SECTION. One of the best-known features of the water system of early Jerusalem is Warren's Shaft. The complex is believed to date from the days of the Kings of Judah, and its purpose was to allow a descent from ground level via a tunnel to a hidden spring. A narrow shaft descends from the surface to a passage with steps leading down to a second shaft, and from there by a horizontal tunnel to the spring. The plan also shows the section made by the English archaeologist Kathleen Kenyon in 1960–1968. The purpose of her dig was to discover the First Temple city walls which pass along the slopes of the city towards the Kedron Valley. The walls seen along the top of the hill were perhaps those built by Nehemiah in the Persian period and refortified by the Hasmonean Kings. These walls stood till the destruction of the Second Temple.

HEZEKIAH'S TUNNEL. Also known as the Siloam Tunnel, Hezekiah's Tunnel still fulfils the same function today as it did when first built in the days of Hezekiah; it carries water from the Gihon Spring in the Kedron Valley to the Pool of Siloam in the Tyropoeon Valley to the west of the Ophel Ridge. In Hezekiah's day the Tyropoeon Valley had already been settled, and of course it was necessary to transport water to this side of the city. Before the Assyrians besieged Jerusalem in 702 B.C.E., the tunnel was started, and work began at both ends simultaneously; the hewers met up somewhere in the middle. A remarkable technical feat, it follows a circuitous course, probably dictated primarily by the various rock formations of the hill.

*The Herodian Pavement and stones
from the destruction of the Temple.*

The Second Temple Period
(538 B.C.E.–70 C.E.)

The accompanying map gives a picture of Jerusalem from the days of Nehemiah (445 B.C.E.) to the Destruction of the Second Temple (70 C.E.). The map is based on the writings of Josephus Flavius and archaeological research of the past century. Josephus describes Jerusalem on the eve of the Roman siege (The Jewish War V 4–5), Herod's rebuilding of Jerusalem (Jewish Antiquities XV, 11; The Jewish War I, XXI, 1), and makes abundant reference to Jerusalem throughout his works. The basis of our knowledge of Jerusalem at this time is generally reliable. Jerusalem's 'overflow' beyond Mt. Ophel can be attributed to the Hellenistic period. It was common at the time for inhabitants to abandon their old towns and rebuild them on nearby sites. In this way the Upper City came into existence on Mount Zion covering the present-day Armenian and Jewish Quarters. Soon it was surrounded by a wall—the location of which has been ascertained by excavations at various points. It was the actual topography of the hills which dictated the development of the city. The major topographical problem of the Second Temple period is the second city wall built apparently by Herod—although certain scholars believe it to have been erected earlier. Its northern gate can be seen underneath the Damascus Gate and the remains in the Russian Church, near the Muristan Quarter, appear to be of this wall.

Our knowledge of the third wall is extensive; it was built by Agrippas, the work was interrupted by the Romans and it was only completed on the eve of the siege. The course of this third wall, parts of which were uncovered by Prof. Sukenik and Prof. Mayer, enlarged the city whose area covered at least two square miles in contrast to the present-day area of much less than a square mile.

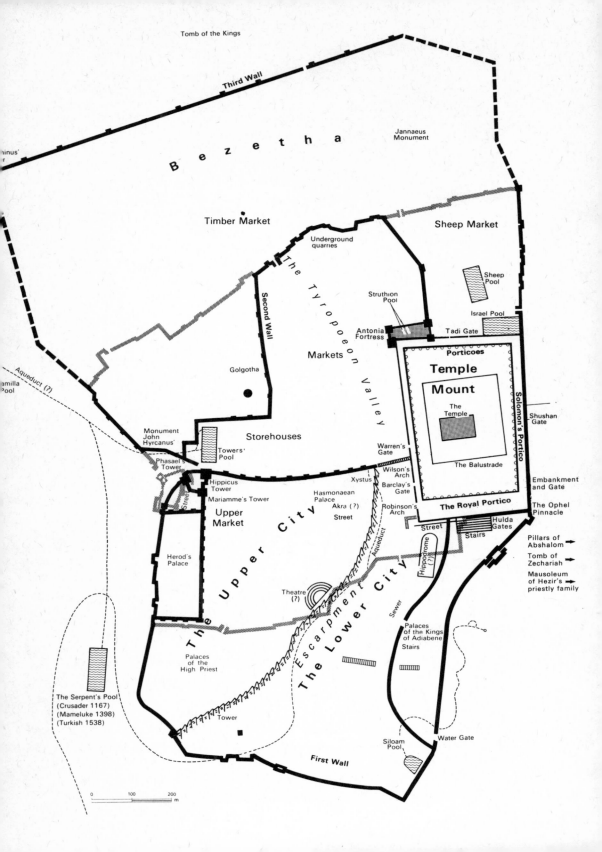

Tomb of the Kings

Third Wall

B e z e t h a

Jannaeus Monument

...minus' ...r

Timber Market

Sheep Market

Underground quarries

Struthion Pool

Sheep Pool

Second Wall

The Tyropoeon Valley

Israel Pool

Antonia Fortress

Tadi Gate

Markets

Porticoes

Temple Mount

The Temple

Shushan Gate

Golgotha

Monument John Hyrcanus'

Storehouses

Towers' Pool

Warren's Gate

Wilson's Arch

Solomon's Portico

The Balustrade

Phasael's Tower

Hippicus Tower

Xystus

Barclay's Gate

Embankment and Gate

...amilla ...ool

Aqueduct (?)

Mariamme's Tower

Hasmonaean Palace

Robinson's Arch

The Ophel Pinnacle

Upper Market

Akra (?)

Street

The Royal Portico

Pillars of Abshalom

Street

Hulda Gates

Herod's Palace

Street

Aqueduct

Hippodrome (?)

Stairs

Tomb of Zechariah

Theatre (?)

The Upper City

Mausoleum of Hezir's priestly family

Sewer

Palaces of the High Priest

The Lower City

Escarpment

Palaces of the Kings of Adiabene

Stairs

The Serpent's Pool
(Crusader 1167)
(Mameluke 1398)
(Turkish 1538)

Tower

Siloam Pool

Water Gate

First Wall

0   100   200
m

Section of the Herodian eastern wall of the Temple Mount.

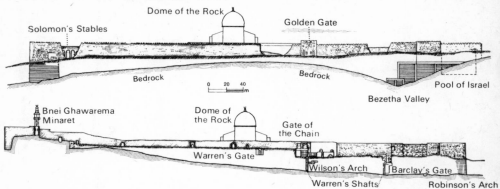

THE TEMPLE MOUNT. *One of the most extensive building projects in the entire history of the Roman Empire was Herod's constructions on the Temple Mount. In order to build his huge platform for the accomodation of the Temple Compound, Herod had a terrace constructed around the hill and this was filled in with rubble—in some places reaching a height of 50 metres. The two streams on either side of the hill—the Tyropoeon Brook and the Brook of Bezetha— were partly blocked up in order to support the platform on which an area of about 250 by 250 metres was demarcated for the sacred precincts.*

Herod built two citadels at key points in the city. The first, the Antonia, was located between the Brook of Bezetha and the Tyropoeon Valley and defended both the Temple Mount and the area included within the second wall, while the second was a structure with three towers, one of which, Phasael's Tower (today called David's Tower), protected the western approaches of the Upper City and Herod's Palace to the south. It straddled the watershed between the Valley of Ben Hinnom and the valley which ran along what is today David Street, and is commonly known as the Transversal Valley.

Herod adorned Jerusalem with magnificent buildings, and the zenith of construction in the city was the laying of the majestic quadrangular terrace which formed the Temple Mount enclosure, and the series of colonnades around the Temple Mount. The Temple itself was an unparalleled edifice. Herod also built a theatre and a number of water reservoirs, the most famous of which, still in existence today, are the Serpents' Pool, the Towers' Pool, the Sheep Pool and the Struthion Pool.

Among the inhabitants of the Ophel Hill—the historical core of Jerusalem— was the royal family of the Adiabene Kingdom.

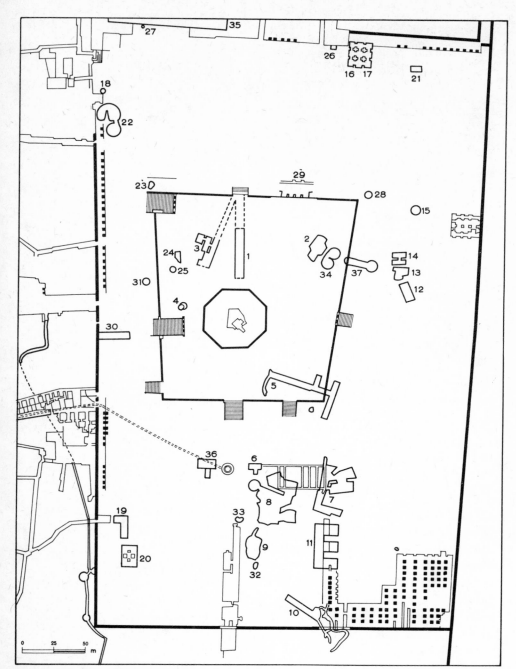

THE CISTERNS ON THE TEMPLE MOUNT. Naturally the water requirements for the Temple were immense, and for this purpose a complex water system was developed. When the terrace of the Mount was constructed and filled in, many empty spaces had been left within the mass for water accumulation. Possibly, during later periods, additional cisterns had been dug on the Temple Mount, but today it is difficult to substantiate this supposition. Almost nothing had been done to further our knowledge of the Temple's water complex since Warren's investigations of the last century. Of particular interest are cisterns number 19–20 and number 30 which had originally been passages to the Temple Mount in the days of the Second Temple, and which were later sealed and used as cisterns; also there is a possibility that no. 1, 3 are remains of passages for priests out of the Inner Temple leading northwards.

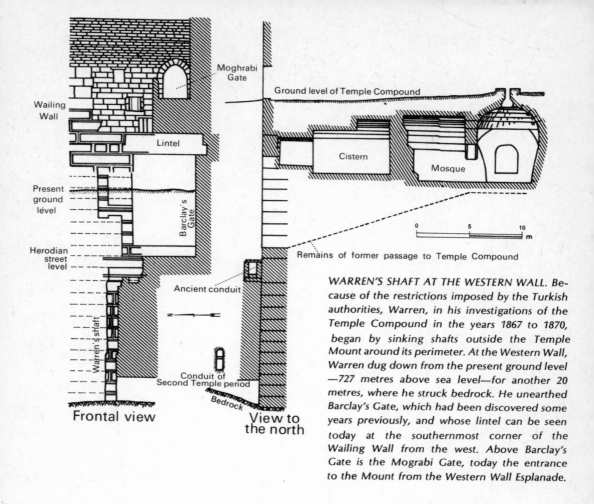

Moghrabi Gate

Ground level of Temple Compound

Wailing Wall

Lintel

Cistern

Mosque

Present ground level

0   5   10
                m

Herodian street level

Remains of former passage to Temple Compound

Ancient conduit

Barclay's Gate

Warren's shaft

Conduit of Second Temple period

Bedrock

Frontal view

View to the north

WARREN'S SHAFT AT THE WESTERN WALL. Because of the restrictions imposed by the Turkish authorities, Warren, in his investigations of the Temple Compound in the years 1867 to 1870, began by sinking shafts outside the Temple Mount around its perimeter. At the Western Wall, Warren dug down from the present ground level —727 metres above sea level—for another 20 metres, where he struck bedrock. He unearthed Barclay's Gate, which had been discovered some years previously, and whose lintel can be seen today at the southernmost corner of the Wailing Wall from the west. Above Barclay's Gate is the Mograbi Gate, today the entrance to the Mount from the Western Wall Esplanade.

THE TOMB OF ABSALOM. The three monuments in the Kedron Valley, opposite the south-eastern corner of the Temple Mount, were all built by wealthy citizens of Jerusalem in the Second Temple period. Of the three only the Tomb of the family of Hezir is positively identifiable as the actual tomb of that family. The most splendid one, the tomb known as the tomb of Absalom, was constructed in the Herodian period. Its lower part, hewn out of the rock, was the burial chamber, while the upper part, which was artificially constructed, constitutes the monument itself. In the course of time this tomb came to be associated with various notables such as the Kings of the House of David, and in the last few hundred years has been popularly identified with Absalom, son of King David. Although still a common belief today, this attribution is unfounded.

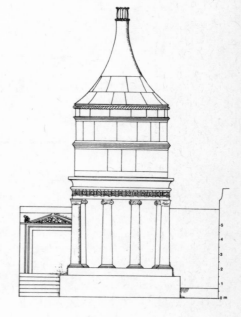

Antonia Fortress area, seen from the Temple Mount. Stonecutting for the construction of the Temple Platform can be clearly seen in the rock face.

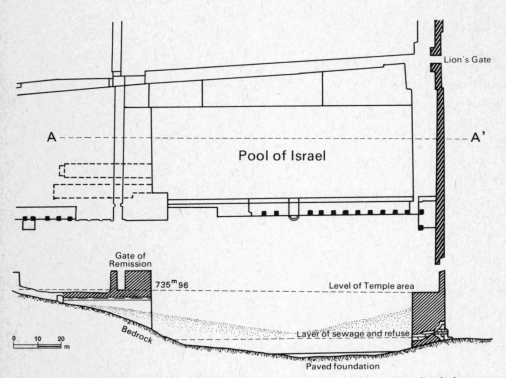

THE BEZETHA BROOK, whose lower section had been filled in when the Temple platform was constructed, had in earlier times served as one of Jerusalem's most important sources of water. Certain sections along its length had been walled up to form pools—the best known are the Sheep's Pool and the Pool of Israel. The latter was the largest of all those within the precincts of the city; its present name is derived from the Arabic. It was about 110 metres in length, 39 metres wide and 27 metres deep with the enormous capacity of some 100,000 cubic metres. In 1934 it was filled in because the water had become contaminated.

Jerusalem in the Time of Jesus

Pool of Bethesda
(Healing of the
Sick Man)

Sheep Gate

Praetorium

Tomb of the
Virgin (?)

Site of Stoning
of Stephen (?)

Grotto of
Affliction

Temple
Mount

Possible Route of Way of the Cross

Golgotha

Tomb of Jesus
(Tomb of Joseph
of Arimathea)

"Judgement Gate"

The Tyropoeon Valley

Solomon's Portico

The Temple

Pinnacle

The Upper City

The Lower City

Escarpment

House of
Caiaphas (?)

Siloam Pool
(Healing of the
Blind Man)

Potter's Field
Burial-Place
of Proselytes

0   100   200
m

In the time of Jesus, the city generally appeared as is shown on the map of Jerusalem at the end of the Second Temple period. The third wall, however, and the suburb of Bezetha included within it, were built some years after his death.

The city which Jesus knew was the Herodian Jerusalem, with its rebuilt Temple Compound. The rebuilding of the Temple and its beautiful appearance are mentioned in the Gospels.

The New Testament is sparing in descriptions of Jerusalem, and generally goes into detail only when the narrative requires it. Usually, it mentions only the name of a place without any distinguishing feature which would help us to identify it at the present day. Moreover, matters are further complicated by the fact that during their periods of domination in the city, Christians built churches and other commemorative buildings on sites of doubtful authenticity which nevertheless, in the course of time, have gained the sanction of tradition.

If we attempt to reconstruct the appearance of the city in the time of Jesus, we must disregard these buildings and the traditions surrounding them, and confine ourselves to the historical sources and archaeological finds. If we do so, the number of holy sites will be drastically reduced, but we will gain a clearer picture of them. Our reconstruction will draw on certain sources: 1) Extra-canonical literary works of the period, such as the writings of Josephus Flavius; with his help we can locate, for example, Solomon's Porch, mentioned in John 10:23 and Acts 3:11 etc. 2) Archaeological excavations, which have yielded evidence concerning, for instance, the pinnacle of the Temple (Matthew 4:5, Luke 4:9), or the Antonia Fortress containing the Pretorium, mentioned several times in the Gospels (there is a relatively exact description in John 19:5-13).

In this map, we have attempted a scientific, though hypothetical, reconstruction of the Way of the Cross. The route which was arrived at is not so very different from the one shown to tourists, which is curious enough in view of the fact that the tradition on which it is based is very late. Generally, we have avoided including in the map places not mentioned in the New Testament or sanctified only by later periods. An exception is the Judgement Gate, today within the Russian Hospice; remains of a gate which could well date from the time of Jesus have been found on this site, giving easy access to the Holy Sepulchre.

We have omitted the Stations of the Cross, because they are merely traditional and lack scientific authentication. This is also true of some other sites, such as the Crusader (or perhaps even Byzantine) remains on Mt. Zion, including the Coenaculum.

With regard to many sites, various churches have conflicting traditions as to where an event took place, which only serves to add to the confusion. The Catholics and Armenians, for example, each claim their own site for the House of Caiaphas, and similar disagreements exist in many other cases.

The "Ecce Homo" Arch.

Aelia Capitolina
(135–330 C.E.)

Josephus relates that when the Temple was destroyed, three towers—Phasael's Tower, Hippicus' Tower and Mariamme's Tower—as well as a section of the wall between the Jaffa Gate of today and the south-west corner, were preserved for the purposes of the 10th Legion (named Fretensis) left behind to garrison the city. To repopulate Jerusalem Titus brought in some 800 service veterans; concurrently, Jews began to return to the city settling presumably in what is today the Jewish Quarter. From a 4th century source we learn that there were seven synagogues in the city—one of them remained intact until that time.

This was the state of Jerusalem when Hadrian visited in the year 129, and he was immediately prompted to rebuild Jerusalem as a Roman city. The building preparations and the inauguration of the city by means of a furrow ploughed around its wall constituted one of the major provocations for the Bar Kochba revolt (132–135 C.E.). Only in the year 136 after the revolt had been suppressed could Hadrian move ahead with his plans for a city that would bear his name—"Aelia Capitolina". ("Aelia": Hadrian's full name was Publius Aelius Hadrianus; and "Capitolina" because of the Capitolina triad: Jupiter, Juno, Minerva, introduced into the city at the time). Most of our knowledge about "Aelia Capitolina" derives from later Christian sources. One source records that the city was divided into seven wards, each headed by a warden after whom each ward was named. According to this same source Hadrian destroyed the Jewish Temple (apparently only what remained of it), built two public bath houses (probably those today called Hamman esh-Shifa and Hamman el-Ain), a theatre and a square-shaped fountain (in all likelihood the pool next to the Siloam Pool). Hadrian thus went on to organize the city along the lines of a typical rectangular Roman town. And this basic shape has persisted through the ages. At the intersection of the two main roads Hadrian built a grandiose tetrapylon, repaired the Temple Mount enclosure (the Quadra) and built a temple to Jupiter on the site where the Temple had stood. In front of the temple to the east he had a statue of himself erected looking eastwards. Two triumphal arches were erected north and west of the city centre.

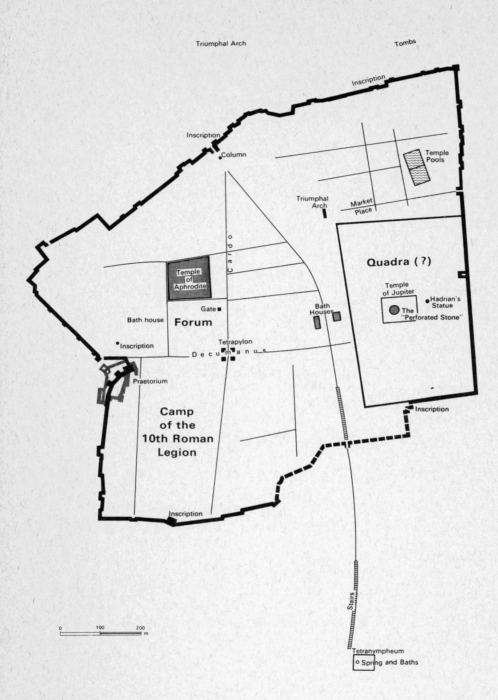

Triumphal Arch   Tombs

Inscription

Inscription

Column

Temple
Pools

Triumphal
Arch   Market
Place

Cardo

Temple
of
Aphrodite

Quadra (?)

Temple
of Jupiter

The
"Perforated Stone"

Hadrian's
Statue

Gate

Bath house   **Forum**

Bath
Houses

Inscription

Tetrapylon

D e c u m a n u s

Praetorium

Inscription

**Camp
of the
10th Roman
Legion**

Inscription

Stairs

Inscription

0   100   200
m

Tetranympheum
o Spring and Baths

0   1   2
m

THE ECCE HOMO ARCH. Theories varied throughout the ages as to the actual route of the Via Dolorosa. But the arch, erroneously called the Ecce Homo Arch, which stands in the street leading from the Lions' Gate, has constantly featured as a definite point on the Via Dolorosa in all the theories. It was commonly believed that this was the place where Pontius Pilate brought Jesus before the people outside the Praetorium, saying "Behold the Man." When the monastery of the Sisters of Zion was built in 1864, part of the arch was incorporated into the new building. Archaeological excavations within the monastery's church, however, revealed that the arch is not from the Second Temple period at all, but is one of a series of Triumphal Arches erected by Hadrian. There is also a recent hypothesis that the area had been a market and this arch stood at its western entrance. In any case it is quite certain that it was in no way connected with the Antonia Fortress in the time of Jesus.

According to Christian tradition, Hadrian built a temple to the goddess Aphrodite at the site of the Holy Sepulchre. South of this temple, in the centre of the city, was the Forum. The encampment of the 10th Legion in the present-day Armenian Quarter was built earlier, during Titus' time, and was organized around two main intersecting roads. At the camp's northern extremity was the Legion's headquarters, making full use of Herod's three towers. Despite many vicissitudes the basic form of Hadrian's city has persisted in the Old City of Jerusalem of today. The most significant archaeological finds from the time are inscriptions foun   at various points:

a) An inscription just east of the Double Gate reads:
"To Titus Aelius Hadrianus Antonius Augustus Pius, the Father of the Fatherland, Pontifex, Augur. By decree of the Decurions."
b) At the base of a column near the Jaffa Gate there is an inscription:
"To Marcus Junius Maximus, Legate of the Emperors in command of the 10th Legion Fretensis Antoniniana. (This stone is erected by) Gaius Domitius Sergianus and Julius Honoratus, his equerries."
c) On the Damascus Gate:
"Colonia Aelia Capitolina, Decuriorum Decreto (. . . by Decree of the Decurions).

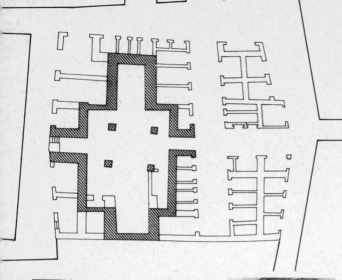

THE MARKET JUNCTION.
At the intersection of the two principal streets of Aelia Capitolina, one running from north to south, and one from east to west, stood a tetrapylon with a facade facing each direction. Still today this intersection is the junction between the Old City's main streets. Today, a cross-shaped Turkish building stands over this site which now serves as a cafe.

Section of the Ecce Homo Arch in the Convent of the Sisters of Zion. It formed part of a triumphal arch in Aelia Capitolina.

Inscription in honour of a commander of the Tenth Legion, Marcus Junius.

Ecce Homo—central archway of Aelia Capitolina triumphal arch.

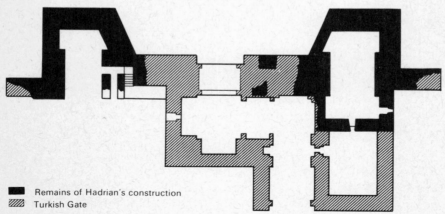

■ Remains of Hadrian's construction
▨ Turkish Gate

THE DAMASCUS GATE was built by the Sultan Suleiman the Magnificent on the site of a Roman gate which appears to have been built when the city was fortified in the third century. It could also perhaps have been a freestanding structure, possibly a triumphal arch dating from 136 C.E. when Aelia Capitolina was founded. The large central arch is flanked by two smaller ones and was built out of stones taken possibly from an earlier nearby building. Close by, remains of a Herodian gate have also been found.

23

The Double Gate.

The Byzantine Period
(330–640 C.E.)

One of the most important sources of information on Jerusalem during the Byzantine period is the 6th century Madaba Map. This famous mosaic map was based on earlier sources, mainly Christian, dating from the era of Christian predominance which lasted till the 7th century.

Jerusalem is portrayed large, on an approximate scale of 1:1,600, and is termed "the Holy City of Jerusalem." The city does not differ much, in general, from how it appeared after Hadrian. Two roads running along its length and one along the width divide the city into several quarters. At the centre of the map is the main transversal street, colonnaded on either side, which terminates at an open space with a column; (even today the Damascus Gate is known in Arabic as "the Gate of the Column"). The Church of the Holy Sepulchre built by the Emperor Constantine is the most prominent building in the city and in the map one can even discern the stairway ascending from the road to its three entrances, as well as the golden cupola above the Sepulchre itself. The Tower of David and another tower, both built by Herod, can also be clearly seen. Similarly, the large church which was on Mt. Zion (where today the Church of the Dormition stands), is clearly visible. Some scholars claim that the Western Wall appears on this map, as a large masonry mass at the southwest extremity of the Temple Mount. If so, this is the first time that the Western Wall is depicted on a known map.

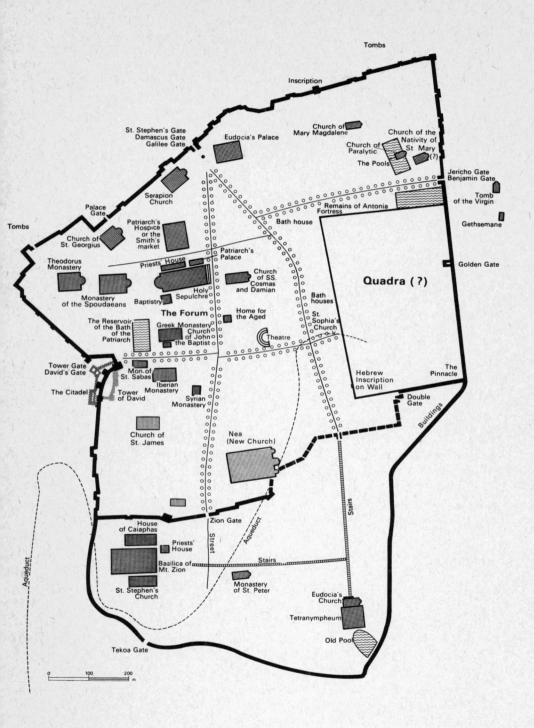

Tombs

Inscription

St. Stephen's Gate
Damascus Gate
Galilee Gate

Eudocia's Palace

Church of
Mary Magdalene

Church of the
Nativity of
St Mary
(?)

Church of
Paralytic

The Pools

Jericho Gate
Benjamin Gate

Tomb
of the Virgin

Serapion
Church

Palace
Gate

Gethsemane

Remains of Antonia
Fortress

Tombs

Church of
St. Georgius

Patriarch's
Hospice
or the
Smith's
market

Bath house

Golden Gate

Theodorus
Monastery

Priests' House

Patriarch's
Palace

Quadra (?)

Monastery
of the Spoudaeans

Baptistry

Holy
Sepulchre

Church
of SS.
Cosmas
and Damian

Bath
houses

The Reservoir
of the Bath
of the
Patriarch

The Forum

Home for
the Aged

St.
Sophia's
Church

Greek Monastery
Church
of John
the Baptist

Theatre

Tower Gate
David's Gate

Mon. of
St. Sabas

Iberian
Monastery

Hebrew
Inscription
on Wall

The Pinnacle

The Citadel

Tower
of David

Syrian
Monastery

Double
Gate

Buildings

Church of
St. James

Nea
(New Church)

Stairs

Zion Gate

Aqueduct

House
of Caiaphas

Priests'
House

Street

Basilica of
Mt. Zion

Stairs

St. Stephen's
Church

Monastery
of St. Peter

Eudocia's
Church

Tetranympheum

Aqueduct

Tekoa Gate

Old Pool

0   100   200
m

The Double Gate—a 6th century Byzantine addition to the Second Temple Ḥulda Gate.

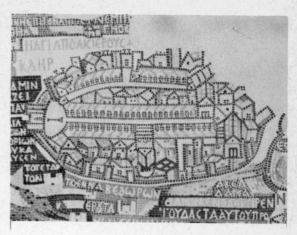

Section of Madaba Map showing 6th century Jerusalem.

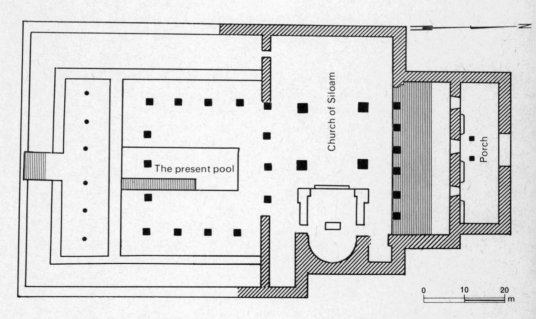

THE SILOAM POOL. Traditionally the Christians hold this pool, which is as old as Jerusalem itself, sacred, as, according to tradition, it was here that Jesus healed the blind man. To commemorate this event the Empress Eudocia built a church beyond the pool in the 5th century. From the pool, which was enlarged and surrounded by a shady colonnade, a flight of steps led northwards to the basilica-shaped church, and beyond the church another flight of stairs led upwards to the city. The present pool has been dug out in part of the earlier pool and measures 16 metres in length by 4 metres width.

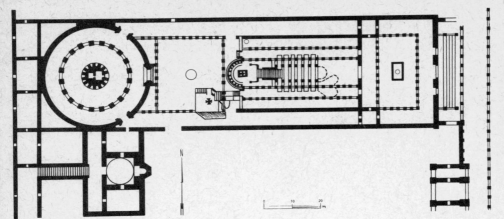

THE CHURCH OF THE HOLY SEPULCHRE. Since Byzantine times this church has been the most significant building in the city. Erected by the Emperor Constantine when his mother Helena discovered the site of the Holy Cross, this magnificent church was built on the site of Hadrian's temple to Aphrodite. The direction for prayer was westwards—an unusual feature of church architecture. From an open colonnaded courtyard three doorways led into the main church, or Martyrium, which was supported by four rows of columns with prayer niches at its western end. Its size was 26 by 45 metres. In the centre of the hall a flight of steps descended to a chapel named after Helena, and a further flight of steps descended to the spot where she found the True Cross. The church was consecrated in 335 C.E.

The Church led out onto a large colonnaded courtyard, at whose south-west corner was the site of the Crucifixion (Golgotha or Calvary). To the west of the garden was the golden-domed Rotunda, known as the Anastasis, which contained the Holy Sepulchre itself. The whole complex was destroyed in 614 C.E., and the Church as it exists today dates mainly from the Crusader period. Very little of its original Byzantine structure has remained.

When the Empress Eudocia settled in the town in the mid 5th century C.E., Hadrian's city underwent a fundamental change. The Empress reconstructed most of the wall encircling Mt. Ophel and Mt. Zion. (This wall had originally been built during the Second Temple period). The enlargement of the city by means of this wall, which was, incidentally, to survive for a long time, was of great significance as many Christian holy places were now included within the city confines—the Siloam Pool with its church, the Church of St. Peter in Gallicantu, and the Church of St. Mary's of Mount Zion among them. Jerusalem became a centre for Christian pilgrims; they constantly described the city. From their elaborate descriptions we can reconstruct a detailed picture of Jerusalem in the Byzantine period. Later, when Justinian succeeded to the throne in Byzantium—527 C.E.—building began to flourish in Jerusalem once again. To the existing churches: the Church of Eleona on the Mount of Olives, the Church of Gethsemane, the Church of the Tomb of the Virgin, and the church next to the Pool of Bethseda (adjacent to where the Church of St. Anne was later to be built), Justinian added the New Church of the Virgin Mary, located in the Jewish Quarter, remains of which have been uncovered recently.

In 614 Jerusalem fell to the Persians; they put paid to the adorning of the city. Churches were destroyed, monks and clergy were slain, and had it not been for the energetic efforts of the Patriarch Modestus in repairing the damage, Jerusalem would not have regained even part of the splendour that typified her during the Byzantine period.

The Foundation Stone.

The First Moslem Period
(640–1099 C.E.)

During this phase which lasted from the Arab conquest of 640 to the Crusader conquest of 1099, there was no change in the overall aspect of the city. To the Moslems Jerusalem was holy, but they did not regard it as an administrative or political centre, and removed their capital to the Moslem town of Ramla. Shortly after the Moslems had conquered Jerusalem the Caliph Omar paid a visit to the city; he proceeded to clean out the filth and debris that had accumulated over the years on the Temple Mount and converted it into a Moslem place of worship. Thus the foundations were laid for the Al Aqsa Mosque; legend has it that Omar built a mosque next to the Church of the Holy Sepulchre because he did not want to pray within the portals of the church itself. This mosque still exists today. Many of the Christian inhabitants left the city and Moslems, many of whom were of Yemenite origin, settled in their place.

From accounts written by a European traveller who visited Jerusalem in 680 we learn that the el Aqsa Mosque was already in existence; it was a large wooden structure capable of accommodating thousands of people. Consequently, in place of the wooden structure, a new building was constructed, most of which is still extant. The Dome of the Rock was to have been a large monument and was not intended to serve as a place of prayer at all. The tale that the Dome was built in order to divert visitors and pilgrims from the Kaa'ba, the sacred stone in Mecca, evidently originates with the enemies of the Omayyad dynasty during whose reign the structure was built. The Omayyad rulers, and particularly Abd-el-Malik (685–705) did much for the city—the city walls were repaired, access roads were improved and so on.

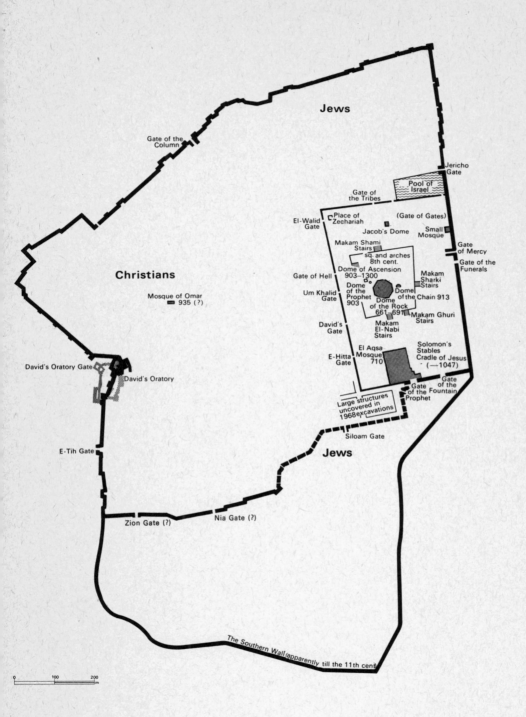

Jews

Gate of the
Column

Jericho
Gate

Pool of
Israel

Gate of
the Tribes

(Gate of Gates)

El-Walid
Gate

Place of
Zechariah

Christians

Jacob's Dome

Small
Mosque

Makam Shami
Stairs

Gate
of Mercy

Mosque of Omar
935 (?)

sq. and arches
8th cent.

Gate of the
Funerals

Dome of Ascension
903–1300

Gate of Hell

Dome
of the
Prophet
903

Makam
Sharki
Stairs

Um Khalid
Gate

Dome
of the Chain 913

Dome
of the Rock
661 691

David's
Gate

Makam Ghuri
Stairs

Makam
El-Nabi
Stairs

E-Hitta
Gate

El Aqsa
Mosque
710

Solomon's
Stables
Cradle of Jesus
(—1047)

David's Oratory Gate

David's Oratory

Gate
of the
Prophet

Gate
of the Fountain

Large structures
uncovered in
1968 excavations

E-Tih Gate

Siloam Gate

Jews

Zion Gate (?)

Nia Gate (?)

The Southern Wall (apparently till the 11th cent.)

0   100   200
                m

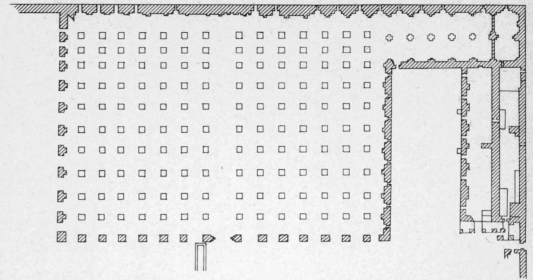

THE EL AQSA MOSQUE. In the Early Moslem period the whole of the Temple Mount was called El Aqsa, meaning 'the distant place' in Arabic, for this spot was traditionally held to be the destination of Mohammed's Night Journey recorded in the Koran. As a result, the city of Jerusalem and this site in particular became one of the holiest places of Islam. Built over the remains of the Second Temple Hulda Gates, the El Aqsa Mosque's foundations are consequently insecure and the building has frequently been the victim of natural disasters. It was first constructed by el-Walid al-Malik in 715 C.E. In 746 it was destroyed by an earthquake, and in 780 it was rebuilt by the Abbasids. Again in 985 it was destroyed. With the coming of the Crusaders it became a church and the headquarters of the Templars, who called it the Temple of Solomon, and held it till Saladin conquered Jerusalem. In 1936 an earthquake again undermined its foundations, and the building has since been continually renovated. In its present form it is a mixture of all the styles that have gone into its making.

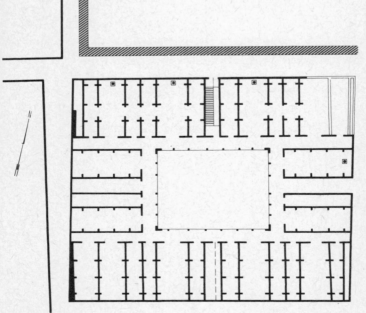

THE OMMAYYAD BUILDINGS. The remains of four large Early Moslem buildings have been uncovered in Prof. Mazar's excavations around the Walls of the Temple Mount since the Six Day War. These are thought to have been part of the Temple Mount's complex of religious buildings; one has been ascertained as the palace of the Omayyad Caliphs, and one served perhaps as living-quarters for the religious functionaries; the purpose of the other two is still unclear. The plans of all the buildings are similar: each has a series of rooms divided into three units, all grouped around a large central chamber. Examples of this plan have been found throughout the Omayyad world, in Iraq, Syria, etc.

Dome of the Rock—the most important building of the Early Moslem period in Jerusalem. 7th century.

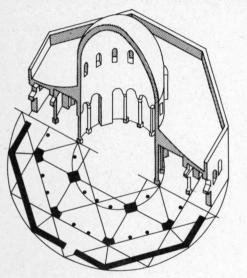

THE DOME OF THE ROCK. An octagonal building on the Temple Mount 21 metres long and 43 metres high is the oldest surviving complete example of early Moslem architecture. It was intended not as a place of worship but as a shrine protecting the Foundation Stone—the rock upon which, according to tradition, Abraham prepared to sacrifice Isaac and which was supposed to have been the site of the Holy of Holies in the First and Second Temples. To Moslems it signified the spot from which Mohammed ascended on his Night Journey. The building was constructed in 691 by Abd-al-Malik and although renovations were made by al-Mamun in the 9th century, and many times since, the building has essentially preserved its original form. Recent renovations during Jordanian rule include the replacement of many of the Turkish tiles on the exterior, and the replacement of the lead dome weighing nearly 200 tons with a dome of aluminium and bronze weighing 35 tons.

But the city suffered severely in the power struggle between the Omayyads (660–750) and the Abbasids (750–969). At the beginning of the 9th century a revolt broke out within the country against the tyrannical rulers, and the inhabitants of Jerusalem were sorely affected. In 868 Palestine was annexed to Egypt by Ahmed ibn Tulun and Jerusalem once more became an important religious centre to which many leading personages from neighbouring countries were brought for burial. The early years of the Fatimid rule (969–1071) were marked by economic prosperity, but soon political hardships led to financial disorders and religious fanaticism, and in their wake synagogues and churches were destroyed by the authorities.

At the beginning of the 11th century Ramla dwindled in significance, presumably as a result of a series of earthquakes which shook the town—and Jerusalem once again spiralled to central position in the country. Towards the close of the Arab period Seljuk tribes began to take an interest in developments in the area, and the city was subjected to incessant conquests, destruction and unrest lasting until the advent of the Crusades.

Church of St. Anne.

The Crusader Period
(1099–1187 C.E.)

Maps, contemporary descriptions and the actual course of the present-day wall—basically the same as that of Crusader days—all teach us of the Crusader city of Jerusalem.

The Crusaders besieged Jerusalem for about a month. Their forces were arrayed on several fronts; in the north was Godfrey of Bouillon (in the vicinity where the Rockefeller Museum now stands), the troops of Robert of Flanders were stationed between Herod's Gate and the Damascus Gate, Robert of Normandy between Damascus Gate and the New Gate and Tancred in the region of Zahal Square; Raymond of St. Gilles had his forces in the area of the Zion Gate. On July 15th 1099, the Crusaders stormed Jerusalem, rapidly overcoming the resistance of the local defenders of the Jewish Quarter (the Moslem Quarter of today).

With the consolidation of their power—an event accompanied by a massacre of the majority of the population—the Crusaders began to resettle the area of the Christian Quarter. Only special tax remissions, property rights and other concessions enabled the Christian population of Jerusalem to increase, while non-Christians—Jews and Moslems—were forbidden to settle, at least in the early years of Christian rule.

Despite the many privileges offered citizens of the Italian city-states they did not settle in the city since they would then have been too far from the sea. The city's economy was based primarily on providing for the needs of the many pilgrims.

Evident in the map are the numerous churches and monasteries established at all sites that were in some way connected with Jesus, his family, the disciples and incidents associated with the lives of other saints.

As a junction between east and west, Jerusalem had many markets, arranged according to the ethnic origin of the merchants—the Syrian market, the Latin market etc.

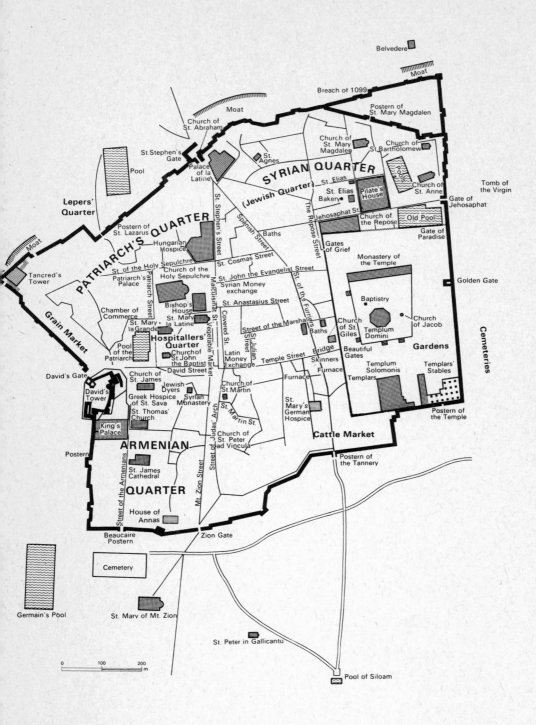

Belvedere

Moat

Breach of 1099

Postern of St. Mary Magdalen

Moat

Church of St. Abraham

St.Stephen's Gate

Pool

Palace of la Latine

St. Agnes

Church of St. Mary Magdalen

Church of St.Bartholomew

SYRIAN QUARTER

(Jewish Quarter)

St. Elias

St. Elias Bakery

Church of St. Anne

Tomb of the Virgin

Lepers' Quarter

Pilate's House

Gate of Jehosaphat

Postern of St. Lazarus

Moat

PATRIARCH'S QUARTER

Hungarian Hospice

Jehosaphat St.

Church of the Repose

Old Pool

Gate of Paradise

St. Stephen's Street

St of the Holy Sepulchre

Baths

Gates of Grief

Monastery of the Temple

Tancred's Tower

Patriarch's Palace

Church of the Holy Sepulchre

St. Cosmas Street

Spanish Street

The Repose Street

St. John the Evangelist Street

Syrian Money exchange

Golden Gate

Patriarch Street

Bishop's House

St. Anastasius Street

St of the Furriers

Baptistry

Church of Jacob

Chamber of Commerce

St. Mary la Latine

Malcuisinat St.

Covered St.

Street of the Marshal

Baths

Templum Domini

Grain Market

St. Mary la Grande

Hospitallers Quarter

Vegetable Market

Church of St. Giles

Gardens

Pool of the Patriarch

Church of St. John the Baptist

Latin Money Exchange

St. Julian Street

Temple Street

Bridge

Skinners

Beautiful Gates

Templars' Stables

David's Gate

David's Tower

Church of St. James

David Street

Jewish Dyers

Church of St. Martin

Furnace

Furnace

Templum Solomonis

Templars

Greek Hospice of St. Sava

Syrian Monastery

St. Thomas' Church

Street of Judas' Arch

St. Martin St.

St. Mary's German Hospice

Postern of the Temple

King's Palace

Church of St. Peter ad Vincula

Cattle Market

Postern

ARMENIAN

Street of the Armenians

Mt. Zion Street

Postern of the Tannery

St. James Cathedral

QUARTER

House of Annas

Cemeteries

Beaucaire Postern

Zion Gate

Germain's Pool

Cemetery

St. Mary of Mt. Zion

St. Peter in Gallicantu

Pool of Siloam

0   100   200
m

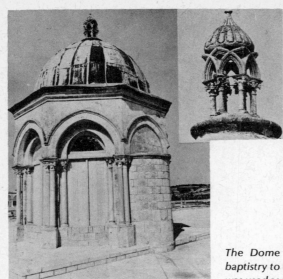

Turret of the Dome of Ascension—one of the high points of Crusader art in Jerusalem.

The Dome of Ascension—the Crusader baptistry to the Dome of the Rock when it was used as a church.

THE DEIR ZEITUNA CONVENT—Convent of the Olive Tree—was so named because it was believed to be the site of the olive-tree to which Jesus was tied when brought to trial at the house of the High Priest Annas, (John 18:13). It acquired its other name—the Angel's Convent —on account of the angels who appeared at the moment when Jesus was struck by the servant of Annas. The present structure dates from the twelfth century, with additions made in 1286 by Levon III King of Armenia.

The various quarters in the city were also organized along ethnic lines: in the present-day Jewish Quarter were Germans, in the Armenian Quarter of today the French residents, and there were also Hungarian, Spanish and English communities in the city.

The Temple Mount became a religious centre, and the Dome of the Rock was renamed "Templum Domini"—Temple of the Lord, and the Al Aqsa Mosque was called "Templum Salomonis"—Temple of Solomon.

The Citadel was fortified anew along Crusader lines, and it still retains the basic Crusader design to this day. Nearby was the palace of the Kings of Jerusalem and the residence of the city's permanent garrison force.

Crusader Jerusalem fell to Saladin in 1187. Only in 1229, under the Emperor Frederick II did Christian rule return to Jerusalem, and even then only for a brief respite of fifteen years.

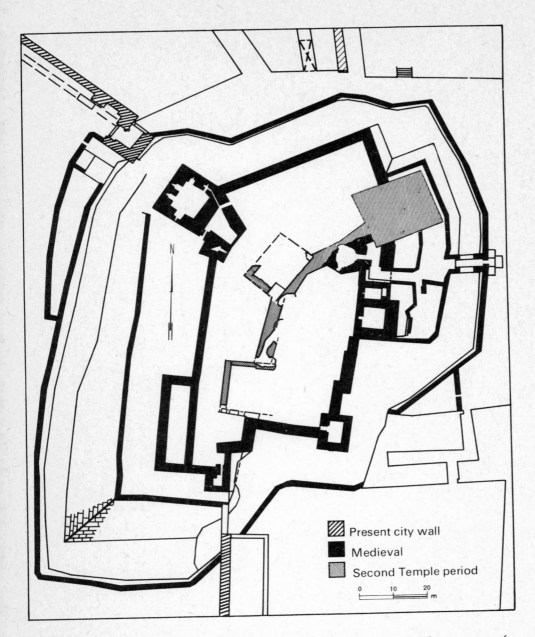

Present city wall

Medieval

Second Temple period

0   10   20
m

THE CITADEL, guarding the western approach to Jerusalem is made up of several towers, one of which dates from the Second Temple period. Ever since Second Temple times a fortress has stood on this site. In time it underwent various changes and its present plan was fixed in the Crusader period when the city's governor and military commanders resided there. In 1217 it was partially destroyed by the ruler Al Muadhdham; it was repaired in 1247 by al-Malek al-Salih Ayyub. Finally the Turkish Sultan Suleiman the Magnificent added the mosque, turret and the front gate to the fortress.

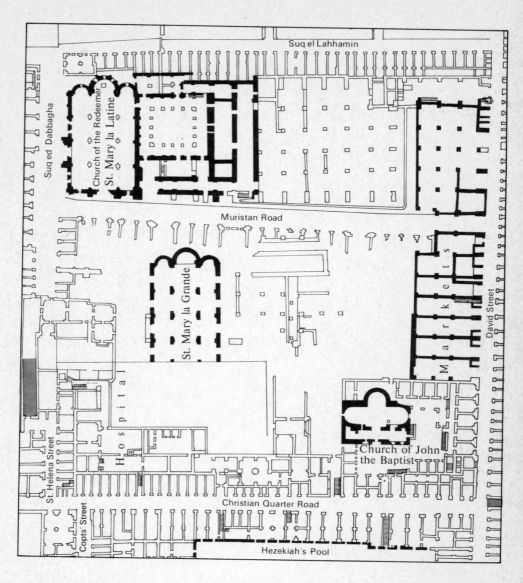

THE MURISTAN. The plan represents the district between David Street and the Church of the Holy Sepulchre. In Roman and Byzantine times the city forum was located in this area which in the Crusader Period was given over to the Knights later known as the Knights of St. John or Knights of Rhodes and Malta. They built a hospital here and thus acquired their name Knights Hospitallers. When Saladin conquered the city, his forces continued to use the hospital and hence the name of the quarter - Muristan, meaning 'hospital' in Kurdish. Later the district fell into decay and in 1864 part of it was given to the Germans who built the Church of the Redeemer on the site of the Crusader church of St. Mary la Latine. The Greeks who owned the western section built their distinctive shopping area here.

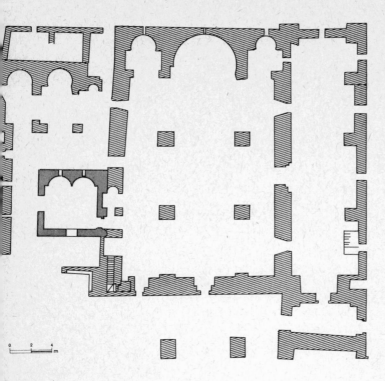

THE ARMENIAN CHURCH OF ST. JAMES. This church stands on the traditional site of the house of St. James the Less, brother of Jesus, whose remains were brought here for burial in the 4th century. Tradition has it that the head of St. James the Great, beheaded by Agrippa in 44 C.E., is also buried here. The site is believed to have housed a place of prayer in the 1st century, but by the 4th century there was probably a church here. This was destroyed in the Persian invasion of 614 C.E. and rebuilt in the 8th century; the Crusaders gave it its final form in the 12th century. Since then it has been lavishly embellished by wealthy patrons and Armenian rulers, and is now the main church of the Armenian community in Jerusalem.

THE TOWER OF GOLIATH. The tower was given its name by the Arabs who believed this to be the historic battle site between David and Goliath. It is also known as Tancred's Tower because it was from this direction that Prince Tancred besieged Jerusalem in 1099 C.E. It was built during the first half of the twelfth century in order to defend the vulnerable north-western corner of the city.

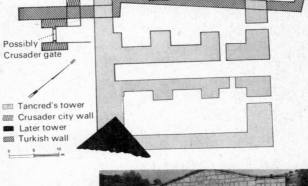

Possibly Crusader gate

▨ Tancred's tower
▧ Crusader city wall
■ Later tower
▨ Turkish wall

0   5   10
m

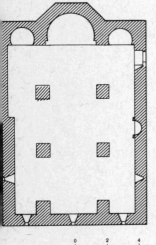

THE CHURCH OF ST. AGNES. This typical 12th century Crusader church stands in the heart of the present-day Moslem Quarter. It is now the Maulawiyya Mosque.

0   2   4
m

Tomb of the Virgin—part of a Crusader church in the Kedron Valley.

0   2   4
m

37

*The carved lions
on the Lions' Gate.*

The Mameluke Period
(1187–1517 C.E.)

After Jerusalem had fallen to Saladin in 1187 the city passed through many hands till its conquest by the Turks in 1517; there were the Christians from 1229 to 1244, the Tatars, Mongols and various Arab rulers (the Ayyubids till 1250 and the Mamelukes till 1453). However, the period is known as the Mameluke era because it was the Mamelukes who exerted the most marked and permanent influence on the city.

Although Saladin was in general exceedingly tolerant of Christian buildings, he did convert the Church of St. Anne into a Madrasa (school) which bore his name—Salahiyya, and built a place of worship not far from the Holy Sepulchre—Khanqah Salahiyya.

The Moslems retained exclusive control of the Holy Places, a measure which proved particularly lucrative when Christian pilgrimages to Jerusalem were resumed at this time.

When Saladin rose to power he repaired the city walls but the Governor of Egypt Malek-el Mu'azzam ordered their destruction in 1219. Under Christian rule the walls were rebuilt again, but they could not withstand the invasions of 1300.

One of the foremost figures in the development of the city was Tankiz, deputy ruler of Syria, who indulged in feverish building activity. One of the most outstanding structures he built was the Tankiziyya (al-Mahkama) 1328–1330. Only Al-Malek-an-Naser surpassed him; he redecorated the mosques of the Haram area and built the Cotton Merchants' Gate.

The Madrasa Baladiyya and the Madrasa Arghuniyya, next to the Iron Gate, and many other schools, built in the latter years of Mameluke rule demonstrate the intention of the Moslem rulers to make Jerusalem a seat of religious learning, rather than a political centre.

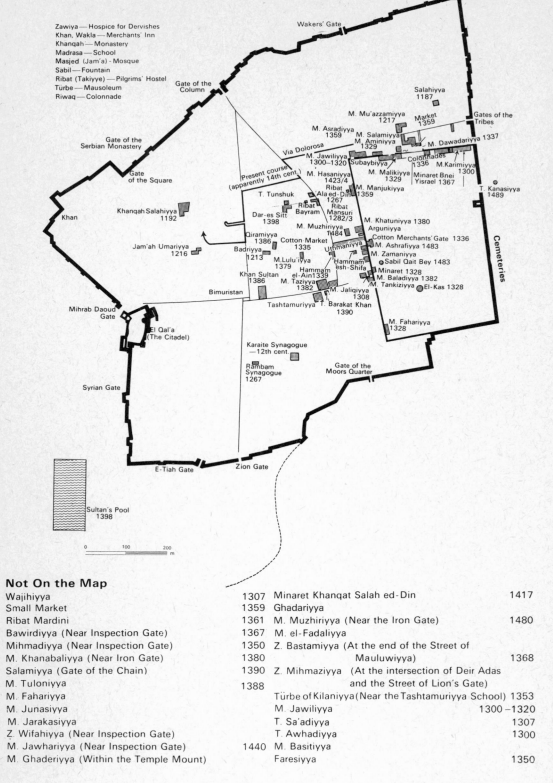

Not On the Map

Entrance to the Madrasa Ashrafiyya, 15th century. One of the most beautiful Mameluke facades.

14th century Tomb of an Uzbek woman. Street of the Chain.

From the rule of Malek edh-Dahr Barquq towards the close of the 14th century till the beginning of the 15th century, the city enjoyed a further spate of development; the Khalidiyya Library and Turbe (mausoleum) of Barakat Khan, in the alley leading to the Western Wall, were built, the Sultan's Pool was renovated, and the aqueduct from Solomon's Pool was repaired. One of the latest projects undertaken by the Mamelukes was that of Qait Bey, who built a magnificent fountain on the Temple Mount.

The Mamelukes devoted most of their efforts to embellishing the Haram Esh Sharif and its surroundings. The city wall and its fortifications, which had last been renovated by Saladin, were dilapidated—the moats had been used for growing vegetables, and the stones had been reused for new buildings.

Jews now played a distinguished part in city life. Already in the 13th century there was immigration to Palestine; Jews came from France and at the end of the century Nahmanides settled in the country, focusing Jewish interest in Jerusalem. The Crusaders had decimated the Jewish population of Jerusalem and ever since the community had remained small.

In the 14th century Eshtori Haparchi immigrated to Jerusalem, but later left because of dissension which erupted in the city between different Jewish communities. Many travellers have related that Jews served as their guides in the city. In the 15th century the Jews figured pre-eminently in Jerusalem. We know that at this time there was a synagogue on the Street of the Jews.

Just prior to the Turkish conquest, which followed shortly after the expulsion of the Jews from Spain, there was a large scale Jewish immigration to Palestine.

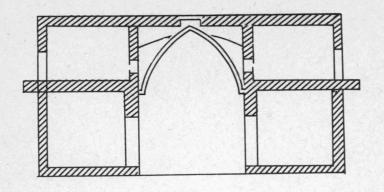

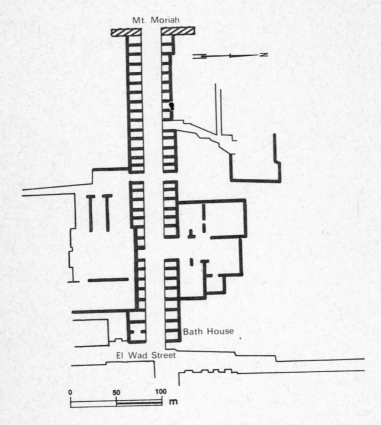

Mt. Moriah

Bath House

El Wad Street

0   50   100
m

THE COTTON MERCHANTS' MARKET. *This Market is witness to the fact that Palestine, like other oriental countries, became a centre of the cotton trade in the Mameluke period. Built by the Emir Saif ed-Din Tankiz in 1336, it was placed under the authority of the Supreme Moslem Council, and the profits went towards the upkeep of the Temple Mount and the Khanqah Salahiyya school. The Market building consists of two rows of shops and adjacent courtyards used for beasts of burden. During the Turkish period it fell into disrepair and attempts to restore it by the Turks in 1898 and by the British in 1923 were unsuccessful. The building itself is almost un-adorned except for the splendid gateway leading to the Temple Mount.*

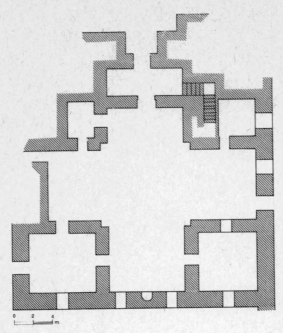

THE TANKIZZIYYA. *This building stands in a typically medieval court-yard in front of the Gate of the Chain surrounded by other Mameluke buildings. Built originally as a school by Seif ed-Din Tankiz in 1328, it soon became the city's civil law courts which it remained until the end of the Turkish period. Hence it came to be known as al-Mahkama (law court). The Jews believed it originated in the Chamber of Hewn Stone (the seat of the Sanhedrin) of the Second Temple period. Today the building serves as a high school.*

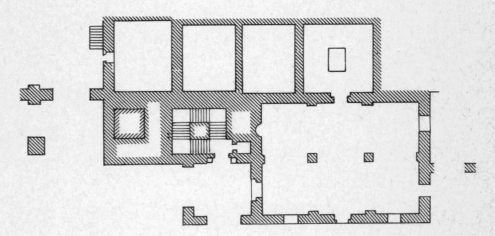

THE ASHRAFIYYA. *This school on the Temple Mount was originally built by the Emir Hassan ed-Dahari and handed over to Qait Bey, after whom the school was named. It served to house Sufi dignitaries. In 1475 it was demolished but rebuilt in 1480. Considered in its time the third most beautiful building on the Temple Mount, it is certainly one of the best examples of Mameluke architecture in Jerusalem.*

42

FOUNTAIN OF QAIT BEY 19th century wood engraving

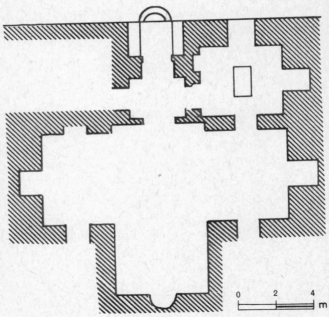

THE ARGUNIYYA. This religious academy was completed in 1358, a year after the death of Arghun al Kamali, governor of Syria, who was buried here in October 1357. It stands in one of the most interesting streets in the city, which still retains its original medieval appearance and includes several schools and mausoleums, all in the ornamental style widespread throughout the Middle East during the Mameluke period.

43

The Jaffa Gate

The Turkish Period
(1517–1917 C.E.)

In December 1517 the Turkish Sultan Selim I conquered Jerusalem, but it was during the reign of his successor, Suleiman the Magnificent, that the city was vastly improved and took on an aspect of splendour. Suleiman the Magnificent's first project was the improvement of the water supply to the city. In 1532 he repaired the aqueduct which conducted water from Solomon's Pools to the Temple Mount as well as the Sultan's Pool (named after him) as evidenced by the inscription engraved on the fountain above the pool. He built three other fountains; in the small square in front of the Gate of the Chain, at the entrance to the street of the Inspection Gate and in Hagai Street, south of the Cotton Merchants' market. Immediately afterwards Suleiman began to build the city walls. From the inscription above some of the gates we know that the wall was begun in the north, and from there—about a year later—the stonelayers moved to the west and to the east, finishing off in the south (1536–8).

After the death of Suleiman the Magnificent Jerusalem declined, and its population decreased—in the 16th and 17th centuries there were only 10,000 inhabitants. A small garrison billeted in the Citadel and the Turkish governor, resident at the Jawaliyya, were the only evidence that the city was part of the vast empire.

Contemporary travellers describe its sorry state with the narrow streets and abandoned houses on the brink of collapse. The buildings and walls erected by Suleiman lost their splendour, a number of residential areas were reduced to open fields, and thieves terrorized the populace.

It was only in the days of the Egyptian Governors Mohammed Ali and Ibrahim Pasha (1832–1840) that the city was once again brought to order. Restored security made it possible for Christians to renovate their churches outside the city wall, and allowed for the building of Jewish suburbs beyond its confines. It is estimated that at the beginning of the 19th century there were 6,000 inhabitants in the city.

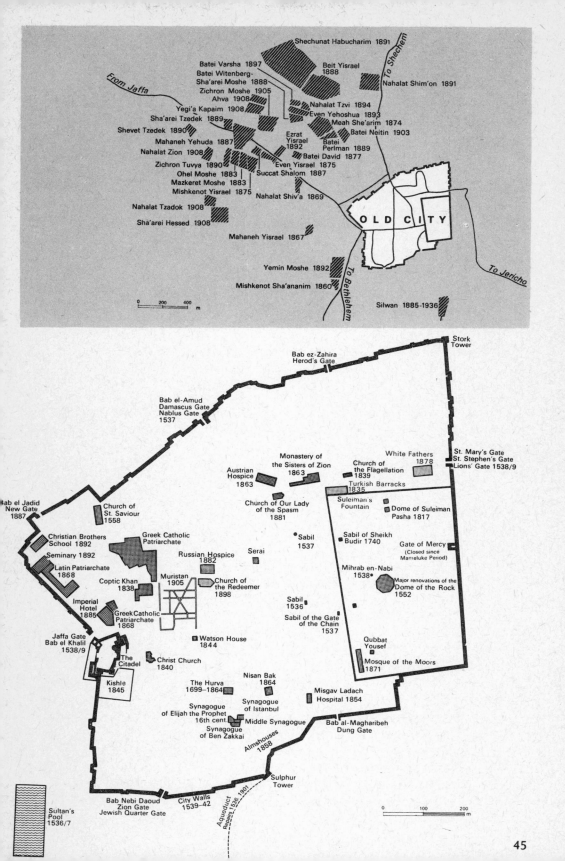

Shechunat Habucharim 1891

To Shechem

Batei Varsha 1897
Batei Witenberg-
Sha'arei Moshe 1888
Zichron Moshe 1905
Ahva 1908
Yegi'a Kapaim 1908
Sha'arei Tzedek 1889
Shevet Tzedek 1890
Mahaneh Yehuda 1887
Nahalat Zion 1908
Zichron Tuvya 1890
Ohel Moshe 1883
Mazkeret Moshe 1883
Mishkenot Yisrael 1875
Nahalat Tzadok 1908
Sha'arei Hessed 1908

From Jaffa

Beit Yisrael 1888

Nahalat Shim'on 1891

Nahalat Tzvi 1894
Even Yehoshua 1893
Meah She'arim 1874
Batei Neitin 1903
Ezrat Yisrael 1892
Batei Perlman 1889
Batei David 1877
Even Yisrael 1875
Succat Shalom 1887

Nahalat Shiv'a 1869

OLD CITY

Nahalat Tzadok 1908

Mahaneh Yisrael 1867

To Bethlehem

Yemin Moshe 1892

Mishkenot Sha'ananim 1860

To Jericho

Silwan 1885-1936

0   200   400   m

Stork Tower

Bab ez-Zahira
Herod's Gate

Bab el-Amud
Damascus Gate
Nablus Gate
1537

Monastery of
the Sisters of Zion
1863

White Fathers
1878

St. Mary's Gate
St. Stephen's Gate
Lions' Gate 1538/9

Austrian
Hospice
1863

Church of
the Flagellation
1839

Turkish Barracks
1835

Suleiman's
Fountain

Dome of Suleiman
Pasha 1817

Bab el Jadid
New Gate
1887

Church of
St. Saviour
1558

Church of Our Lady
of the Spasm
1881

Sabil
1537

Sabil of Sheikh
Budir 1740

Gate of Mercy
(Closed since
Mameluke Period)

Christian Brothers
School 1892

Greek Catholic
Patriarchate

Serai

Russian Hospice
1882

Mihrab en-Nabi
1538

Major renovations of the
Dome of the Rock
1552

Seminary 1892

Latin Patriarchate
1868

Coptic Khan
1838

Muristan
1905

Church of
the Redeemer
1898

Sabil
1536

Imperial
Hotel
1885

Greek Catholic
Patriarchate
1868

Sabil of the Gate
of the Chain
1537

Jaffa Gate
Bab el Khalil
1538/9

Watson House
1844

Qubbat
Yousef

The
Citadel

Christ Church
1840

Mosque of the Moors
1871

Kishle
1845

Nisan Bak
1864

The Hurva
1699-1864

Misgav Ladach
Hospital 1854

Synagogue
of Istanbul

Synagogue
of Elijah the Prophet
16th cent.

Middle Synagogue

Bab al-Magharibeh
Dung Gate

Synagogue
of Ben Zakkai

Almshouses
1858

Sulphur
Tower

Sultan's
Pool
1536/7

Bab Nebi Daoud
Zion Gate
Jewish Quarter Gate

City Walls
1539-42

Aqueduct
Repairs 1536, 1901

0   100   200   m

The peaceful situation that prevailed and the growth of the city's Jewish population brought about the move to settle beyond its boundaries. At first it was difficult to persuade Jews to abandon the safety of the walled city. But in 1865 the first Jewish suburb outside the walls, Mishkanot Sha'ananim, was founded, and the suburbs of Mahaneh Yisrael and Nahalat Shiva were set up in 1868. In this period the population of Jerusalem totalled 18,000, half of whom were Jews. In 1871 Meah Shearim was built and was soon followed by many other suburbs.

The Jewish population increased steadily till the outbreak of the First World War, during which many Jews were expelled, recruited to the army or forced to flee the country.

When the British took the city in December 1917 there were more than 30,000 Jews in Jerusalem out of a total population of 60,000.

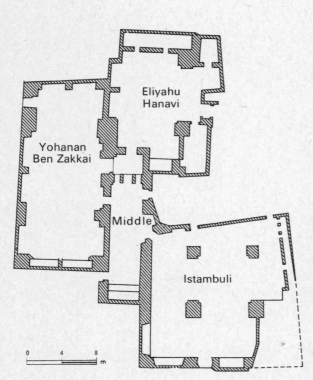

Eliyahu
Hanavi

Yohanan
Ben Zakkai

Middle

Istambuli

0   4   8
m

SYNAGOGUES. After the Turkish conquest, Jews who, prior to their stay in Istanbul, had been expelled from Spain began to arrive in Jerusalem. Almost immediately they set about building synagogues. Four Sephardi synagogues became the centre of the Sephardi community and all four were known as the Ben Zakkai Synagogue; each individual synagogue also bore its own separate name. The complex was demolished during Jordanian rule of the city and was only restored in 1972 and is now once again in use.

The synagogues clearly reveal their architectural origins, particularly the one called the Istanbul Synagogue which is clearly reminiscent of certain buildings in Turkey of the same period. The building is square-shaped with four central pillars supporting the domed exterior. The Ben Zakkai Synagogue is thought to have been constructed on the ruins of a Crusader church; an unusual feature is its two Arks of Law. The Eliahu Hanavi Synagogue, built in the same style as the Istanbul, has preserved certain traditional relics, such as the chair Elijah the Prophet was supposed to have sat in, etc. The Middle Synagogue was a later addition and its construction sealed the space between the larger ones.

CITY GATES. The Turkish city gates such as the Lions' Gate, Jaffa Gate and Damascus Gate, were built over the very site of Roman gates. The Turkish Zion Gate, however, was not in quite the same position as the Roman Zion Gate. These gates constitute a unique example of 16th century Turkish civic architecture, their characteristic features being rosette decorations and historical and religious inscriptions in decorative frames. All the gates were constructed so that one could only enter obliquely, but today some have been modified to allow for motorised traffic.

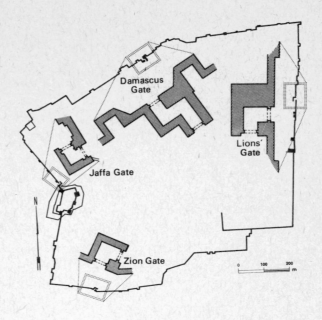

Public fountain at the Gate of the Chain, one of three erected by Suleiman the Magnificent.

Southern view of the citadel, showing the turret of the Turkish mosque.

4

Memorial to the fallen British soldiers.

Jerusalem During the British Mandate
(1921 –1948)

The British Army formally entered Jerusalem on December 11, 1917, led by General Allenby, inaugurating 30 years of British rule. A pressing task for the conquerors was to assure a steady supply of water, and a pipeline was laid to bring water from Solomon's Pools, south of Bethlehem.

The city began expanding rapidly, and water supply continued to be a major problem till, in 1924, the springs in Wadi Kelt were tapped and in 1934 the sources of the Yarkon River were harnessed.

Jerusalem was made the administrative centre of all Palestine and Transjordan. Initially, the High Commissioner had his headquarters at Augusta Victoria on the Mount of Olives but, in 1931, after a period in the city itself, he moved to his permanent abode at Government House on the Mount of Evil Counsel, south of the city.

The city itself was administered by an appointed municipal council. Throughout the British mandate, the Mayor was nominated from among the influential Arab families, even though the majority of the population was Jewish. The Municipal Council was composed of six Jews and six Arabs—of the latter, two Christians and four Moslems.

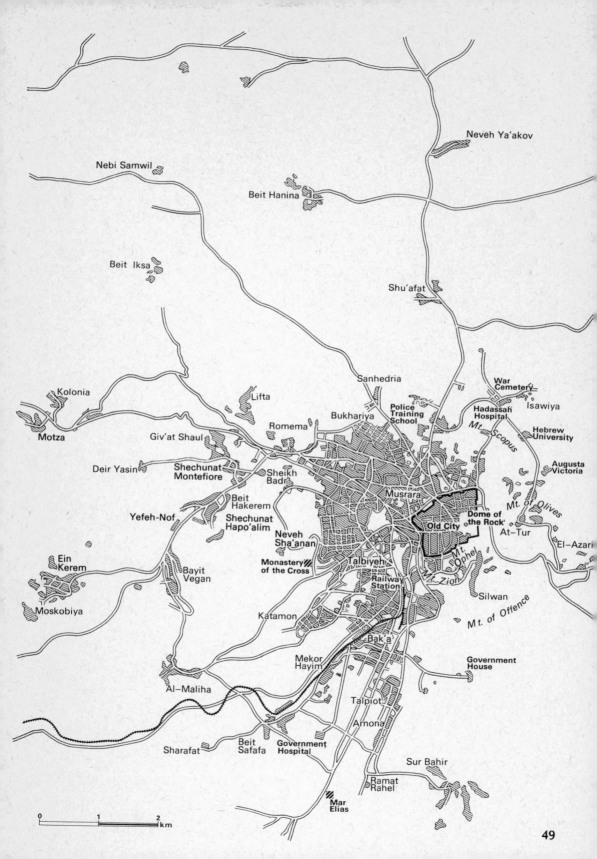

Neveh Ya'akov

Nebi Samwil

Beit Hanina

Beit Iksa

Shu'afat

War
Cemetery

Kolonia

Lifta

Sanhedria

Hadassah
Hospital

Isawiya

Motza

Giv'at Shaul

Romema

Bukhariya

Police
Training
School

Mt. Scopus

**Hebrew
University**

Deir Yasin

**Shechunat
Montefiore**

Sheikh
Badr

**Augusta
Victoria**

**Beit
Hakerem**

Musrara

Mt. of Olives

Yefeh-Nof

**Shechunat
Hapo'alim**

Old City

**Dome of
the Rock'**

At-Tur

El–Azari

**Ein
Kerem**

Bayit
Vegan

Neveh
Sha'anan

**Monastery
of the Cross**

Talbiyeh

*Mt.
Ophel*

Silwan

Moskobiya

Railway
Station

Mt. Zion

Katamon

Mt. of Offence

Bak'a

Mekor
Hayim

**Government
House**

Al–Maliha

Talpiot

Arnona

Sharafat

Beit
Safafa

**Government
Hospital**

Sur Bahir

Ramat
Rahel

Mar
Elias

0   1   2
|————————|————————| km

General Allenby on the steps of the Citadel of Jerusalem requesting the representatives of the local population to preserve the sanctity of the holy sites.

The centre of town housing the main administrative buildings, fortified by the British towards the end of the Mandate. This compound was popularly known as Bevingrad. Note the architecture typical of the period.

Development began immediately upon the establishment of civilian rule and, by 1922, new suburbs had been founded, such as Beit Hakerem and Talpiot. Many of the inhabitants who had formerly lived in the Old City moved to the newly-founded quarters. Some 14,000 Jews lived in crowded conditions in the Jewish Quarter of the Old City towards the end of the Ottoman period. But by 1931 there were only 5,600. At the end of British rule only 2,000 remained. Not only did official institutions leave the Old City (especially from the vicinity of the Citadel), but also the foreign consulates moved their premises, mainly to the south-western suburbs of the new city. The various religious institutions also followed this trend, as did schools and hospitals of all the communities. Jewish expansion was mainly to the west, while Arab development tended to be north of the Old City, in the Bab ez-Zahira and Sheikh Jarrah quarters. Considerable Arab building activity, however, did take place to the south in Bak'a along Hebron Road and in Talbiyeh.

The commercial centre of the city also shifted in Turkish times. Since antiquity it had been located amongst the markets within the Old City, and in the 1920's it spread out along Jaffa Road from Jaffa Gate to the new centre of town around Zion Square. The principal government institutions also came to be situated here: the Main Post Office, Broadcasting House and the Courts were set up in the Russian Compound. This latter area was largely sealed off by the British authorities in 1946, in a closed area (known popularly as "Bevingrad", after the name of the then British Foreign Secretary), thus further separating the main Jewish business centre from the Arab commercial centre.

Heavy industry was discouraged in Jerusalem and the city's economy was based on services, on a large army and police sector, on various religious institutions, on Jewish and other national institutions—all requiring a considerable bureaucracy which lent a particular flavour to the character of the citizenry.

In April of 1920, the first Arab riots took place; major recurrences broke out in August 1929 and in the Arab Insurrection of 1936–39. In Jerusalem hostility was particularly rife, the city representing a religious and political focus for both peoples.

In effect, the city came to be divided into Jewish and Arab sectors even prior to the United Nations vote for the Partition of Palestine, on 29 November, 1947. Clashes and sniping between the factions were a daily occurrence, with contact between the two zones limited to a bare minimum.

At the close of the British Mandatory period, the population of Jerusalem numbered 165,000 of whom 100,000 were Jews, 40,000 Moslems and 25,000 Christians.

*East wing of the Monastery of Notre Dame
destroyed in the 1948 fighting.*

Jerusalem Divided
(1948–1967)

On November 29th 1947 the U.N. resolved to partition Palestine and internationalise Jerusalem. The resolution was accepted by the Jews but rejected by the Arabs. Fighting broke out the following day and terrorism spread against the Jews. Siege, destruction and hunger were once more Jerusalem's lot. The Transjordanian Arab Legion invaded the Old City of Jerusalem.

Before the fighting stopped almost a year later, the Jewish Quarter of the Old City was destroyed and its inhabitants driven out by the Jordanian Army. Mt. Scopus, a vital medical and educational focus, became an isolated enclave severed from the city. Its hospital and university remained closed until 1967.

Areas of no-man's land were marked out (22.7.48) and on 30.11.48 a local commanders' agreement (between Israel and Jordan) was signed in Jerusalem calling for a total cease-fire which came into force on April 3rd 1949. But the agreements were only partially observed; sniping and clashes were Jerusalem's fare in ensuing years. Jordanian soldiers frequently shot at Israeli civilians near the border.

Now Jerusalem, once capital and heart of the country, became a border town at the end of a narrow cul-de-sac, connecting Jerusalem to Israel's population centres on the coastal plain.

From 1948 to 1967 the two sectors of Jerusalem were cut off from one another by barbed wire and minefields with essentially no contact between them. Only diplomatic and church personnel could cross the lines freely, and non-Jewish tourists were allowed to cross from east to west. All such traffic was funnelled through a single control point—Mandelbaum Gate. Jordan denied Jews access to the Western Wall and Israeli Moslems could not visit their shrines in the Old City.

In December 1949 Jerusalem for the third time in history became the capital of Israel and the city began to be rehabilitated. A large campus of Government offices was built and, nearby, the Knesset (Parliament) was completed. A new Hebrew University campus and National Library were built at Givat Ram

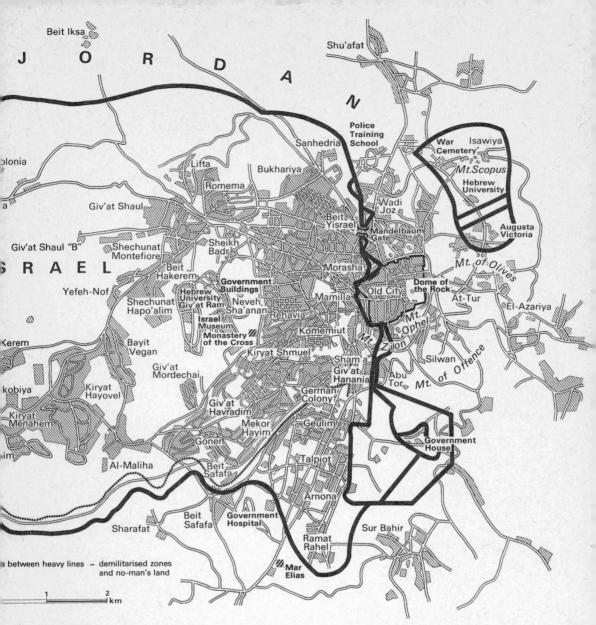

Beit Iksa

J O R D A N

Shu'afat

Police Training School

Sanhedria

War Cemetery   Isawiya

Mt. Scopus

Lifta
Bukhariya
Romema

Hebrew University

Giv'at Shaul

Wadi Joz

Augusta Victoria

Giv'at Shaul "B"

Shechunat Montefiore
Sheikh Badr

Beit Yisrael
Mandelbaum Gate

Mt. of Olives

Beit Hakerem

Morasha

Yefeh-Nof

Government Buildings

Dome of the Rock

Old City

At-Tur   El-Azariya

Hebrew University Giv'at Ram
Neveh Sha'anan

Mamilla

Shechunat Hapo'alim

Rehavia

Israel Museum
Monastery of the Cross

Komemiut

Mt. Ophel

Kerem

Bayit Vegan

Kiryat Shmuel

Mt. Zion

Giv'at Mordechai

Sham'a
Giv'at Hanania

Abu Tor

Silwan

Mt. of Offence

kobiya

Kiryat Hayovel

German Colony

Giv'at Havradim

Government House

Kiryat Menahem

Mekor Hayim

Geulim

Goneni

Al-Maliha

Beit Safafa

Talpiot

Arnona

Sur Bahir

Sharafat

Beit Safafa
Government Hospital

Ramat Rahel

s between heavy lines — demilitarised zones and no-man's land

Mar Elias

|——1——|——2——| km

instead of the ones seated on Scopus. Similarly, a new Hadassah Hospital was erected and became the most advanced medical centre in the Middle East. Suburbs were built to house refugees from quarters of Jerusalem which remained in Arab hands, new immigrants, survivors of the Nazi holocaust and Jewish refugees from Arab countries. On a hill overlooking the city the Yad Vashem memorial and archive was founded in tribute to the victims of the holocaust. The founder of Zionism—Herzl—was buried nearby.

Despite such rapid development, Jewish Jerusalem suffered the tribulations of a divided city. The borders which enclosed West Jerusalem on three sides allowed for expansion only to the west, where the mountainous terrain presented either steep slopes or creviced wadis. The new quarters were now distant from the business centre in the east. There was little space suitable for the industry vital for a city of this size, but light industry began to develop at the end of Jaffa Road, in Romema and Givat Shaul.

The number of inhabitants did increase but not as much as in the rest of the country and Jerusalem, formerly the second largest city, now dropped to third place.

At the close of the 1948 war, there remained 65,000 inhabitants in the Jordanian occupied sector of Jerusalem, more than half of them living within the Old City. Stagnation set in, and by 1967 there were still less than 66,000 inhabitants, about 25,000 living within the Old City proper. The Christian community had shrunk to about 10,800. The main factor for this slowdown was the official Jordanian economic policy which placed emphasis on the development of the East Bank of the kingdom at the expense of the West Bank in general and Jerusalem in particular, with a definite policy of anti-Christian discrimination.

East Jerusalem too was restricted topographically and could develop only towards the north, along the road to Ramallah. Building increased somewhat in the vicinity of the American Colony, as well as in more remote suburbs such as El-Azariya (Bethany) and Abu Dis. The commercial centre of the Jordanian-occupied sector sprang up along Saladin Road, opposite Herod's Gate.

The Arab sector of Jerusalem continued to serve as a local focus for the West Bank although rivalled by Nablus. It was the seat of the Moslem courts, of numerous church functionaries and various religious educational institutions. There were also religious and archaeological research facilities. Christian tourism to the Holy Places became a major economic factor in Jordanian occupied Jerusalem. There the souvenir industry and services of the tourist trade became the main sources of income.

The division of Jerusalem had its physical aspects as well, for along the dividing line rose huge ugly concrete screening walls as protection against Arab sniping, and extensive no-man's land areas, mined and crisscrossed with barbed wire, gashed across the very heart of the city, separating the two sectors.

Partition wall erected after the War of Independence between the two sectors of the town to guard against sniping. The wall was pulled down in 1967 after the Six Day War.

View from Mt. Scopus.

Jerusalem Reunited
(since 1967)

One of the most significant results of the Six Day War of 1967 was the emotional impact of the reunification of Jerusalem. For the Jews, access was once again restored to the Temple Mount, the Western Wall and the Jewish Quarter of the Old City, and Moslems and Christians were ensured free access to their shrines. Shortly after the war, the walls and fences cleaving the city were dismantled, and it again became one. There was an immediate improvement in Municipal services, such as a secure water supply in the eastern parts of the city. Better sanitation and full employment gave a new look to the city. Streets which had been truncated were now rejoined and refurbished and development begun. Debris heaped up against the Old City walls was largely removed, and a park has since taken its place. Almost all war damage has since disappeared.

New Jewish suburbs have been developed on the hills surrounding the city, and the modern Arab quarters, such as Wadi Joz and Shu'afat, have resumed expansion. Jewish and Arab construction witnessed a tremendous upsurge. The Hebrew University campus and Hadassah Hospital on Mount Scopus have been massively rebuilt to serve the entire city.

The reunification of Jerusalem has restored the city to its natural position as the focal point of the country. Expansion has been rapid: at the time of the reunification, there were 196,000 inhabitants in the Israeli sector and 66,000 inhabitants in the Jordanian sector, totalling 262,000 inhabitants. By 1976 there were 256,000 Jews and 96,000 Moslems and Christian inhabitants, making Jerusalem the largest municipal entity in Israel. The non-Jewish inhabitants comprise about a quarter of the city's population.

The Knesset (Parliament) built in the sixties. In the foreground is the Shrine of the Book which houses the Dead Sea Scrolls. Both are part of a complex of public buildings which includes the Givat Ram campus of the Hebrew University, Kiryat Ben-Gurion (government city) and the Israel Museum.

Many Jewish families from other parts of the country have flocked to the city as have Jewish new immigrants. Standards of living and incomes have risen. Traffic in the city's streets has increased beyond all estimates. Yet the economic base of the city in either part has not been affected greatly by the reunification and the proportion of clerical and other institutional workers remains high.

Jerusalem is the principal centre of archaeological research in the country and more of the city's past has been revealed in the last 7 years than by all the work of the past hundred years. A remarkable feature has been the integration of the archaeological excavations and reconstruction with the development of the Jewish Quarter.

The Wolfson Towers—a newly built residential quarter in the west of town. 1975-76.